chinese cooking
made easy

simple and delicious meals in minutes

Discover how easy it is to create mouth-watering Chinese dishes in your own kitchen. Chinese cooking can be easy as most ingredients can be readily purchased from supermarkets, and even online! This book features a selection of over 55 delicious Chinese dishes that are easy to prepare at home, and light and healthy too.

D1511057

TUTTLE PUBLISHING
Tokyo • Rutland, Vermont • Singapore

Contents

MAIL ORDER SOURCES

Finding the ingredients for Asian home cooking has become very simple. Most super-markets carry staples such as soy sauce, fresh ginger, and fresh lemongrass. Almost every large metropolitan area has Asian markets serving the local population—just check your local business directory. With the Internet, exotic Asian ingredients and cooking utensils can be easily found online. The following list is a good starting point of online merchants offering a wide variety of goods and services.

http://www.asiafoods.com
http://www.geocities.com/MadisonAvenue/8074/VarorE.html
http://dmoz.org/Shopping/Food/Ethnic_and_Regional/Asian/
http://templeofthai.com/
http://www.orientalpantry.com/
http://www.zestyfoods.com/
http://www.thaigrocer.com/Merchant/index.htm
http://asianwok.com/
http://pilipinomart.com/
http://www.indiangrocerynet.com/
http://www.orientalfoodexpress.com/

Introduction

What is the reason for the enduring worldwide popularity of Chinese food? It begins with a cornucopia of unique ingredients, vegetables and nourishing tofu, plus sauces and seasonings that are partnered with just about every creature that swims the seas, flies the air or roams the land. This astonishing variety of ingredients is transformed by the Chinese into memorable works of culinary art. Every dish must meet three criteria—appearance, fragrance and flavor; other considerations are texture, the health-giving properties of the food and its auspicious connotations.

The array of seasonings and sauces used by Chinese cooks is not vast; nor are a large range of culinary techniques employed. However, the endless interplay of one basic ingredient with another—meat with tofu, vegetables with slivers of pork—and the transformation of these basics when combined with different seasonings, allows for almost endless variety.

The most essential utensil in Chinese cooking is the wok—a parabolic pan traditionally made of cast iron and used for just about everything except cooking rice: stir-frying, deep-frying, braising, making sauces, holding a steaming basket and so on.

Claypots of various shapes and sizes are used for slow cooking and for making soups and stocks. These are attactive and inexpensive, but any type of saucepan could be used instead.

Steaming is a healthy method of cooking favored by the Chinese, who traditionally use a multi-tiered bamboo steamer with a woven cover that absorbs any moisture, unlike a metal cover where moisture condenses and then falls back onto the food. The steaming basket is placed inside a wok, sitting a few inches above the boiling water.

Stir-frying is by far the most commonly used method. Other simple methods include steaming, braising, deep-frying and slow cooking.

Timing is absolutely crucial to the success of Chinese dishes. Most food is cooked very briefly, so it is essential to chop all the ingredients, measure all the seasonings, and have garnishes and serving dishes ready before starting to cook. Control of heat is also important, and for this reason, a gas flame is far superior to any other form of heat. Make sure you prepare and place the ingredients near the stove in order of use. And remember, as any Chinese cook would agree, practice makes perfect.

Basic Chinese Ingredients

Black bean paste is a richly-flavored seasoning made from soybeans, similar to Japanese miso (which may be used as a substitute). The beans are fermented and salted and sold in jars. They vary in color from dark brown to light golden. The basic black bean paste contains only soybeans, water and salt. It is also possible to buy slightly sweetened versions or those with added chili. The beans are usually mashed with the back of a spoon before use.

Black Chinese vinegar is made from rice, wheat and millet or sorghum. The best black vinegars are aged and have a complex, smoky flavor similar to balsamic, which may be substituted. Chinese cooks add black vinegar sparingly to sauces, dips and when braising meats.

becued meats. Store in the refrigerator after opening.

Dried chilies

Finger-length chilies

Bird's-eye chilies

Chili peppers come in many shapes, sizes and colors. Fresh green and red Asian **finger-length chilies** are moderately hot. **Dried chilies** are usually deseeded, cut into lengths and soaked in warm water to soften before use. **Ground red pepper**, also known as cayenne pepper, is a pungent red powder made from ground dried chilies. Substitute dried red chili flakes or chili paste. **Chili oil** is made from dried chilies or chili powder infused in oil, which is used to enliven some Sichuan dishes.

Black Chinese mushrooms, also known as *shiitake* mushrooms, are used widely in Chinese cooking. Dried ones must be soaked in hot water to soften before use, from 15 minutes to an hour depending on the thickness. The stems are removed and discarded; only the caps are used. Substitute porcini mushrooms. Fresh *shiitake* are widely available in many supermarkets now.

Bok choy is a highly nutritious variety of cabbage with long, crisp stalks and spinach-like leaves. It has a clean, slightly peppery flavor and is a wonderful addition to soups and stir-fries. It is available in many large supermarkets.

Bottled sweet chili sauce is a commercial blend of chili, vinegar, garlic and salt. Usually used as a dipping sauce, it can also be used on noodles and bar-

Chinese cabbage, also

known as Napa cabbage, has white stems that end in tightly packed pale green leaves. It has a mild, delicate taste.

Coriander leaves (also known as cilantro or Chinese parsley) are used as a herb and a garnish in Chinese cooking. Sold in bunches in the herb section of supermarkets.

Dried shrimp are tiny, orange shrimp that have been dried in the sun. They come in various sizes. Available in Asian markets, they should be orange-pink in color and plump; avoid any with a grayish appearance or an unpleasant smell. Dried shrimp will keep for several months in a sealed container.

Dried sweet Chinese sausages (*lap cheong*), are thin, sweet Chinese pork sausages delicately perfumed with rose-flavored wine. They are used as an ingredient in stir-fries or braised dishes rather than being eaten on their own like European sausages. Sold in pairs, they keep almost indefinitely without refrigeration. Substitute sweet Italian sausage.

Garlic chives, also known as Chinese chives, have thin flat leaves that resemble thin spring onions. They have a strong garlicky flavor and are added to noodle or stir-fried dishes during the final stages of cooking. If you cannot get them, use spring onions or regular chives.

Green onions, also known as scallions or spring onions, have slender stalks with dark green leaves and white bases. They are sliced and sprinkled generously on soups and used as a garnish in Chinese cooking.

Hoisin sauce consists of fermented soybeans, sugar, garlic, chilies and vinegar. The sauce is thick and dark and has a sweet, salty flavor. Commercially bottled or canned hoisin sauce is available in many grocery stores.

Rice vinegar is made from glutinous rice and has a mild, sour flavor. It is colorless and is one of the definitive ingredients used in sweet and sour sauce. Substitute mild white wine vinegar.

Rice wine or sake adds a sweet, subtle flavor to dishes. It is widely available in the specialty food sections of supermarkets. Dry sherry makes a good substitute.

Fresh wheat noodles

Fresh *kway teow* noodles
(*hor fun*)

Dried egg noodles

Noodles are a universal favorite in Chinese cooking. Both fresh and dried noodles are made from either wheat, rice or mung bean flour. **Fresh wheat noodles** are thick, spaghetti-like noodles made from wheat flour and egg. Substitute fresh spaghetti or fettucini if you cannot find them. **Fresh kway teow noodles** (also known as "river noodles" or *hor fun*) are wide, flat rice noodles sold fresh in Asian markets. If not available, use dried rice stick noodles instead. **Egg noodles,** like pasta, are made from wheat flour, water and egg. They are available both fresh or dried. Substitute with ramen noodles, which are dried Chinese-style wheat noodles. They are most commonly available in the form of instant noodles.

Salted black beans are soybeans that have been fermented and preserved in salt, hence their strong, salty flavor. Mainly used to season meat or fish dishes, they are sold in packets or cans and will keep for several months if stored in the refrigerator. Soak in warm water for 30 minutes before using to remove some of the salt.

Salted pickled mustard cabbage (*Kiam chye*) is a type of pickled vegetable like sauerkraut. Soak the salted cabbage in water for 15 minutes to remove some of the saltiness.

Sesame oil is extracted from sesame seeds that have been toasted, producing a dark, dense and highly aromatic oil that is used for marinades, sauces and soups, or as a table condiment. Its nutty, smoky flavor has become a hallmark of north Chinese cuisine.

Sichuan peppercorns are not really pepper but a tiny, reddish-brown berry with a strong fragrance and acidic flavor. Also known as Chinese pepper or flower pepper (*hua jiao*), it has a sharp pungency that tingles and slightly numbs the lips and tongue, an effect known in Chinese as *ma la* "numb hot." Japanese *sansho* pepper, sold in small bottles, contains other ingredients, but has a similar flavor. To obtain **ground Sichuan pepper**, simply dry-roast the peppercorns, then grind to a fine powder in a blender.

Soy sauce is brewed

Soft tofu   Firm tofu   Pressed tofu   Tofu skin

Tofu or beancurd comes in various forms. **Soft tofu** is silky and smooth but difficult to cook because it falls apart easily. **Firm tofu** holds its shape well when cut or cooked and has a stronger, slightly sour taste. **Pressed tofu** (often confusingly labeled as firm tofu) is a type of firm tofu that has had much of the moisture pressed out of it and is therefore much firmer in texture and excellent for stir-fries. Refrigerate fresh tofu submerged in water in a plastic container. **Tofu skin** is the dried skin that forms on top of boiling soy milk; it is dried and sold in sheets.

from soybeans and wheat fermented with salt.
Regular or **light soy sauce** is very salty and is used as a table dip and cooking seasoning. **Dark soy sauce** is denser and less salty and adds a smoky flavor to dishes.

Star anise is a dried brown flower with 8 woody petals, each with a shiny seed inside, which gives a flavor of cinnamon and aniseed. Use whole and remove from the dish before serving. It is available in plastic packets in the spice section of Asian markets and well-stocked supermarkets.

Water chestnuts are small, acorn-shaped roots with a brown leathery skin outside and a crisp, crunchy flesh and a juicy sweet flavor inside. Fresh water chestnuts can be found packed in water in the refrigerator sections of Asian supermarkets. Canned water chestnuts are commonly available.

Wonton wrappers are made from wheat dough,

and come in a variety of sizes and thicknesses. They are filled with meat or vegetables, then steamed, fried or used in soups. Fresh or frozen wonton wrappers are available in many supermarkets.

Wood ear fungus, also called wood ear mushrooms, have little flavor and are added to dishes for their chewy texture and as a meat substitute. They are sold dried in plastic packets in Asian supermarkets and comes in small, crinkly sheets. Soak them in water before using. Wash well and discard any hard bits that remain after soaking.

Chili Garlic Sauce

5 red finger-length chilies
3 cloves garlic
3 tablespoons rice vinegar
1 teaspoon sugar
$1/_2$ teaspoon salt

1 Process all the ingredients in a blender until smooth. Store refrigerated in a dry, covered jar until ready to use. Serve with steamed poultry or rice, and use this as a dip with Lettuce Cups with Mushrooms and Tofu (recipe on page 13).

Yields $1/_4$ cup (60 ml)
Preparation time: 10 mins

Hunan Chili Relish

5 red and 5 green finger-length chilies
5 cloves garlic
1 onion
1 tablespoon oil
$1/_4$ teaspoon salt

1 Coarsely chop the chilies, garlic and onion.
2 Heat the oil and stir-fry the chopped ingredients for 1 minute. Add the salt and serve warm, or at room temperature as an appetizer, or as an accompaniment to Classic Fried Rice (recipe on page 44).

Yields 2 cups (500 g)
Preparation time: 5 mins
Cooking time: 1 min

Chinese Chicken Stock

3 lbs (1.5 kg) chicken bones or $1/_2$ chicken
2 in (5 cm) fresh ginger, peeled and sliced
3 green onions (scallions)
1 stalk fresh celery, leaves attached, roughly chopped
1 teaspoon white peppercorns
10 cups (2.5 liters) water

1 Combine all the ingredients in a large stock pot and bring to a boil over high heat. Reduce the heat and simmer for 1 hour. Discard the solids and strain the stock through a fine sieve. The stock can be frozen for up to 3 months.

Yields 8 cups (2 liters)
Preparation time: 5 mins
Cooking time: 1 hour 10 mins

Spicy Cabbage Pickles

1 small Chinese (Napa) cabbage
2 teaspoons salt
3 red finger-length chilies, deseeded and thinly sliced
1 in (2.5 cm) fresh ginger, peeled and grated
4 tablespoons sugar
4 tablespoons rice vinegar
1 tablespoon oil

1 Wash and dry the cabbage leaves. Slice the leaves into thin ribbons and place them into a bowl. Sprinkle with the salt, mix and set aside for 1 hour.
2 Drain the cabbage of any excess liquid, squeezing gently, and place it in a clean bowl. Add the remaining ingredients, except the oil and mix well.
3 Heat the oil and pour it over the cabbage. Store in a dry, glass container in the refrigerator and marinate for 2 days before consuming. Serve as a side dish with Classic Chinese Egg Rolls (recipe on page 10).

Yields 4 cups (900 g)
Preparation time: 1 hour 10 mins + 2 days marinating time

Crispy Fried Shallots

6–8 small shallots, peeled and thinly sliced
$1/2$ cup (125 ml) oil

Yields 3 tablespoons
Preparation time: 5 mins
Cooking time: 10 mins

1 Heat the oil in a skillet or wok over medium heat and stir-fry the shallots until golden brown, taking care not to burn them as this makes them taste bitter. Remove from the oil and drain on paper towels. If not using them immediately, allow to cool, then store in an airtight jar to preserve their crispness.
2 Reserve the **Shallot Oil** for frying or seasoning other dishes.

Seasoned Sliced Chilies

10–15 bird's-eye chilies, deseeded and thinly sliced
2 tablespoons soy sauce
2 tablespoons lime juice

1 Combine the chilies, soy sauce and lime juice in a small bowl and serve with Claypot Chicken Rice (recipe on page 43).

Yields $1/4$ cup (60 g)
Preparation time: 5 mins

Classic Chinese Egg Rolls

20 spring roll wrappers
1 egg, beaten
Oil, for deep-frying
Bottled plum sauce, to
  serve
Hot Chinese or English
  mustard, to serve
Spicy Cabbage Pickles
  (page 9), to serve

Filling
1 teaspoon cornstarch
1 teaspoon soy sauce
1$^1/_4$ cups (250 g) ground
  pork, or diced ham
2 tablespoons oil
$^1/_2$ cup (75 g) thinly sliv-
  ered bamboo shoots
2 carrots, peeled and
  grated
2 cups (180 g) thinly sliced
  Chinese (Napa) cabbage
2 green onions (scal-
  lions), sliced
2 cups (100 g) fresh bean
  sprouts
1 teaspoon salt
$^1/_4$ teaspoon pepper

1 To make the Filling, blend the cornstarch with the soy sauce and combine with the pork. Set aside.

2 Heat the oil in a wok and stir-fry the pork until it changes color, about 3 minutes. Add the bamboo shoots and carrot, and stir-fry for 2 more minutes.

3 Add the cabbage and stir-fry for about 2 minutes, or until the cabbage is soft but still crisp. Remove from the heat and stir in the rest of the ingredients. Drain the filling before using.

4 Lay a spring roll wrapper on a clean flat surface, with a corner facing you. Spoon 2 tablespoons of the Filling onto the wrapper, about 2 in (5 cm) from the bottom corner. Shape the Filling into a long, narrow strip.

5 Fold the bottom corner up and over the Filling, and roll once, away from you. Dab the left and right corners with some egg and fold inwards, pressing to seal. Dab the top corner with a bit of egg and roll, sealing the egg roll. Repeat to make more rolls.

6 Heat the oil in a wok over high heat until almost smoking. Add 5 egg rolls at a time and fry until crisp and golden, about 3 minutes. Remove the egg rolls with a slotted spoon and drain on paper towels. Serve with plum sauce, mustard and Spicy Cabbage Pickles.

Makes 20 egg rolls
Preparation time: 30 mins
Cooking time: 30 mins

Fold the bottom corner of the spring roll wrap-per up and over the filling and roll once.

Dab a bit of beaten egg on the left and right corners, then fold them in, pressing to seal.

Lettuce Cups with Mushrooms and Tofu

A quick, fresh appetizer that's fun to eat! The filling has a delicate crunchy texture and a touch of sweetness. These tasty cups can also be made with ground turkey or pork, in place of the tofu.

6 dried black Chinese mushrooms, soaked in warm water for 20 minutes, tough stems discarded and caps diced
2 tablespoons oil
1 cake (10 oz/300 g) firm tofu, cubed
2 cloves garlic, minced
1 tablespoon grated ginger
1 tablespoon rice wine or sake
1 teaspoon sesame oil
$1/4$ teaspoon ground black pepper
1 carrot, peeled and diced
$1/2$ cup (90 g) diced water chestnuts
1 head Butter or Red Leaf lettuce, leaves washed and patted dry
Sliced green onions (scallions), to garnish
Sesame seeds, to garnish
Hoisin sauce, to dip
Chili Garlic Sauce (page 8), to dip

1 Drain the mushrooms, reserving $1/4$ cup (60 ml) of the soaking liquid.

2 Heat 1 tablespoon of the oil in a wok, add the tofu and fry until light brown on all sides, about 5 minutes. Remove, drain on paper towels and set aside.

3 Heat the remaining oil in a wok over medium-high heat. Add the mushrooms, garlic, ginger and rice wine, and stir-fry for 30 seconds. Add the sesame oil and black pepper, and stir-fry for 2–3 minutes, then add the reserved mushroom soaking liquid and diced carrot, and stir-fry for 2 minutes. Stir in the water chestnuts and mix thoroughly.

4 Fill each lettuce leaf with 2–3 tablespoons of the filling. Garnish with some green onions and sesame seeds. Serve with dipping bowls of hoisin sauce and Chili Garlic Sauce on the side.

If using ground turkey or pork in place of the tofu, omit step 2 and stir-fry 1 cup (250 g) fresh ground turkey or pork at the beginning of step 3 until the meat is browned, then continue with the remaining steps.

Serves 4–6
Preparation time: 30 mins
Cooking time: 7 mins

Pot Sticker Dumplings (Guo Tieh)

Pot Stickers are the classic northern Chinese dumplings—first fried in oil then steamed, all in the same pan. The recipe given here use ground pork, but they may also be prepared with vegetables, lamb, chicken or fish.

15–20 round wonton wrappers
1 tablespoon oil, for frying
1 tablespoon plain flour mixed with 1 cup (250 ml) water

Filling
4 dried black Chinese mushrooms, soaked for 20 minutes, tough stems discarded and caps diced
1 1/2 cups (300 g) ground pork, chicken or lamb
3 garlic chives, finely chopped
3 slices fresh ginger, finely minced
1 teaspoon salt
1 teaspoon ground black pepper
1/2 tablespoon sugar
1 tablespoon soy sauce
2 teaspoons sesame oil

1 Make the Filling by placing the chopped mushrooms in a large bowl with the ground meat, garlic chives and ginger. Mix well. Add the seasonings and mix well to combine.

2 Lay the wonton wrappers on a floured surface. Place 1 tablespoon of the Filling onto the center of each wonton skin and lightly brush around the edges with water. Fold one side of the skin over the Filling to meet the other side, creating a half moon shape, and press the edges together. Press the bottom of each dumpling down to flatten, so the dumplings can sit upright.

3 Heat the oil in a non-stick pan over medium heat. Gently fry the dumplings until crisp on the bottom, about 3 minutes. Add the flour water to the pan, cover with a lid and let it steam for 10–12 minutes or until the liquid has just evaporated. Transfer the cooked dumplings to a serving platter and serve with various table condiments, such as chili sauce or chili oil, black Chinese vinegar and fresh ginger strips.

Makes 15–20 dumplings
Preparation time: **30 mins**
Cooking time: **15 mins**

Place 1 tablespoon of the Filling onto the center of each wonton skin.

Fold one side of the skin over the Filling, creating a half moon shape. Press edges together.

Brush the top of each pancake with sesame oil and sprinkle some green onions and salt on top.

Twist the rolled dough into a spiral, pressing the spiral down onto the palm to flatten it.

Tianjin Style Green Onion Pancakes

This is one of the oldest wheat-based dishes in northern China. The preparation process takes time and patience, but is actually quite easy and the result is always worth the effort. No yeast is required. Follow the instructions carefully and you'll produce a perfect pancake.

2 cups (300 g) all-purpose flour
1 cup (250 ml) hot water
2–3 tablespoons cold water
2 tablespoons sesame oil
12 green onions (scallions), finely chopped
1 teaspoon salt
2 tablespoons oil

Makes 6 pieces
Preparation time: 35 mins
Cooking time: 8 mins

1 Sift the flour into a mixing bowl and pour the hot water into the center of the flour, mixing it quickly with a wooden spoon. Then gradually add the cold water, continuing to mix, until a firm dough is formed. Set aside to rest for 10 minutes.

2 Place the dough onto a clean floured work surface and knead vigorously until it is smooth and pliant, about 10 minutes. Roll the dough into a cylinder and cut it into 6 equal pieces. Use a floured rolling pin to roll each piece into a round pancake about 6 in (15 cm) in diameter. Brush the top of each pancake with some of the sesame oil and sprinkle some green onions and salt on top.

3 Fold each pancake in half, then roll it up into a cigar shape. Pinch the ends closed, hold one end in the palm of one hand and use the other hand to twist the rolled dough into a spiral, pressing the spiral down onto the palm to flatten it.

4 Place each spiral face-up on a floured board and use a floured rolling pin to roll it into a round pancake, about 4 in (10 cm) in diameter. Set each pancake aside after rolling.

5 Heat the oil over medium heat in a non-stick skillet. Fry the pancakes two or three at a time (depending on size of skillet) for 3–4 minutes, shaking the pan frequently to prevent sticking and encourage puffing. Turn once and fry the other side for 3–4 minutes, shaking the pan. When done, transfer the pancakes to a plate covered with paper towels and continue to fry the other pancakes in the same manner. Serve warm as an accompaniment to other dishes.

Boiled Chinese Dumplings (Jiaozi)

Known in Chinese as "water dumplings," they are similar to Italian ravioli, which were no doubt inspired by this original Chinese model. They are easy to make and simple to cook. A bigger batch of the Stuffing may be prepared in advance and kept frozen in the freezer until needed.

25 round wonton wrappers

Stuffing
1$^1/_4$ cups (250 g) ground pork
1 egg, lightly beaten
2 green onions (scallions), finely chopped
2 in (5 cm) fresh ginger, finely chopped
1 teaspoon salt
$^1/_4$ teaspoon ground white pepper
2 cloves garlic, finely minced
$^1/_2$ teaspoon sugar
1 tablespoon sesame oil
1 teaspoon rice vinegar
2 teaspoons soy sauce

Condiments
Black Chinese vinegar
Shredded ginger strips
Chili oil
Soy sauce

Makes 25 pieces
Preparation time: **30 mins**
Cooking time: **10 mins**

1 Put all the Stuffing ingredients in a large bowl. Toss to mix well.

2 Lay the wonton wrappers out on a floured work surface. Place 1$^1/_2$ tablespoons of the Stuffing onto the center of each wonton skin and lightly brush around the edges with water. Fold the edges of the skin together to form a half moon, using your fingers to press the edges firmly to seal the dumpling. Place on a lightly-floured platter and continue until all the wonton wrappers are used up.

3 Bring a large pot of water to a boil and gently lower the dumplings into the water, in small batches of 10 dumplings at a time. 1 cup (250 ml) of cool water should be added to the pot—to allow the water to return to a full boil—each time a batch of dumplings is being lowered into the water. This is to ensure the dumplings are fully cooked. The dumplings are cooked when they float to the surface. Remove with a slotted spoon and transfer to a serving platter that has been smeared with a thin coat of sesame oil to prevent sticking, then continue cooking the remaining dumplings. Serve hot with the various Condiments.

You may also use finely chopped beef, lamb or chicken for the Stuffing. Vegetarians may add finely chopped black Chinese mushrooms caps instead of meat.

Pan-fried Vegetable Buns

A typical northern Chinese dish, these wheat-based buns are stuffed with savory ingredients and fried in a flat pan, and served with various table condiments so diners may adjust the flavor to their own preference. The buns are prepared in advance, then fried prior to serving. Ground lamb, pork or chicken may be substituted in place of dried shrimp. Vegetarians may add finely chopped black Chinese mushroom caps. In cold weather, the dough should be allowed an extra 15 minutes to rise.

1 cup (250 ml) warm water
1 teaspoon yeast powder
1 teaspoon salt
$1/2$ teaspoon sugar
3 cups (450 g) all-purpose flour
Flour, for dusting
1 tablespoon oil, for frying
2 teaspoons plain flour mixed with $2/3$ cup (165 ml) water

Stuffing
$1/2$ head Chinese (Napa) cabbage, finely chopped
3 green onions (scallions), finely chopped
$1/2$ cup (60 g) dried shrimp, soaked in warm water, drained and chopped in a blender
1 tablespoon soy sauce
1 tablespoon sesame oil
2 teaspoons ground black pepper
1 teaspoon salt
1 teaspoon sugar

Serves 4
Preparation time: **45 mins + rising time for dough**
Cooking time: **15 mins**

1 Make a dough by pouring the warm water into a bowl. Add the yeast, salt and sugar, and stir until the sugar completely dissolves. Let it sit for a few minutes to allow the yeast to activate.

2 Sift the flour into a large mixing bowl, add the yeast mixture and mix well until a firm dough is formed. Cover with a damp towel and set aside for 45 minutes to allow the dough to rise.

3 Meanwhile, prepare the Stuffing by combining the cabbage, green onions and dried shrimp in a bowl. Add the seasonings and mix well.

4 Remove the dough from the bowl and placed onto a lightly floured surface. Knead the dough for 5 minutes, then return it to the bowl, cover with a damp towel and set aside to rise for another 30 minutes.

5 When the dough has risen, place it back onto the work surface and knead briefly. With a floured rolling pin, roll it out into a long cylinder about $1^1/4$ in (3 cm) thick. Cut the cylinder into pieces about $1^1/4$ in (3 cm) long and roll each piece into a round flat pancake about 4 in (10 cm) in diameter.

6 Spoon 1 heaping tablespoon of the Stuffing onto the center of each pancake, then pull the edges of the pancake up around the Stuffing to form a bun. Twist the edges together at the top of the bun to seal it.

7 Heat the oil in a non-stick pan over medium-low heat and fry the stuffed buns for about 2 minutes. Pour the flour and water mixture into the pan, cover with a lid and let it steam for 10–12 minutes or until the liquid has just evaporated. Remove from the heat and transfer the buns to a serving platter. Serve hot with various table condiments of your choice.

Cut the roll into pieces about 1¹/₄-in (3-cm) length. Roll each piece into a round flat pancake.

Twist the edges together at the top of the bun to seal it.

Shredded Chinese Chicken Salad

A very tasty way of serving chicken—and it's very easy to prepare. The recipe here comes from the home kitchen of a Shantung family in Taiwan.

4 cups (1 liter) water
3 boneless chicken
  breasts, skin removed
1 cup (50 g) chopped fresh
  coriander leaves (cilantro)
5 cloves garlic, thinly sliced
$^1/_2$ head iceberg lettuce,
  finely shredded

Sauce
2 tablespoons rice vinegar
2 teaspoons sugar
1 teaspoon salt
2 tablespoons sesame oil
3 teaspoons yellow mustard
2 teaspoons soy sauce

1 Bring the water to a boil in a pot. Add the chicken breasts, cover with a lid, lower the heat and simmer for 8 minutes. Turn off the heat and let the chicken poach in the hot water for 12 more minutes. Remove the chicken and set aside to drain in a colander.
2 Place the Sauce ingredients in a bowl and mix well.
3 Finely shred the cooled chicken and place in a large bowl. Add the chopped coriander leaves and garlic. Toss to mix well. Add the Sauce and toss again until the chicken is well coated with the Sauce.
4 Arrange the shredded lettuce on a platter and serve the chicken on the bed of lettuce.

Serves 3–4
Preparation time: 20 mins
Cooking time: 30 mins

Crispy Pork and Shrimp Spring Rolls

2 cups (400 g) ground
  pork
8 oz (250 g) fresh shrimp,
  peeled and deveined
$1/_3$ cup (85 g) grated carrot
$1/_4$ cup (60 ml) water
4 small shallots, chopped
2 green onions (scal-
  lions), thinly sliced
6 water chestnuts, peeled
  and diced
$1/_2$ teaspoon salt
1 tablespoon white pepper
1 egg
1 tablespoon cornstarch
3 sheets dried tofu skin
Oil, for deep-frying
Bottled plum sauce or
  sweet chili sauce, to serve

1 Coarsely grind the pork and shrimp in a blender.
2 Blanch the carrot with the water in a saucepan for 2 minutes, then drain. Add the carrot and the rest of the ingredients, except the tofu skin, oil and sauces, to the pork mixture. Grind until the mixture becomes a paste. Transfer to a bowl.
3 Wipe each tofu sheet with a clean damp cloth, then cut each sheet into 6-in (15-cm) squares. Put a little of the mixture onto the center of each piece of tofu skin, then shape it into a horizontal roll. Tuck in the ends, roll up and press gently to seal.
4 Heat the oil in a wok. Deep-fry the rolls, a few at a time, until golden brown and crisp, 4–5 minutes. Drain on paper towels and serve with bottled plum sauce or sweet chili sauce.

Serves 4
Preparation time: 30 mins
Cooking time: 15–20 mins

Egg Drop Soup

A traditional favorite. Ribbons of cooked egg swirled in a savory stock topped with a handful of green onions.

4 cups (1 liter) Chinese Chicken Stock (page 8) or canned chicken stock
1 tablespoon grated ginger
1 tablespoon soy sauce
1 tablespoon cornstarch, blended with 2 tablespoons water
2 eggs, lightly beaten
Pinch of salt and ground white pepper
4 green onions (scallions), sliced, to garnish

1 Bring the Chinese Chicken Stock, ginger, and soy sauce to a boil in a saucepan. Add the cornstarch mixture, reduce the heat and let the soup simmer.
2 Slowly pour in the beaten eggs, stirring constantly in the same direction. Turn off the heat and season with salt and pepper. Garnish each bowl of soup with a small handful of sliced green onions.

Serves 4
Preparation time: 5 mins
Cooking time: 15 mins

Tofu and Spinach Soup

A pure and simple soup that goes well with any meal.

4 cups (1 liter) vegetable stock or Chinese Chicken Stock (page 8)
1/2 cake (4 oz/125 g) soft tofu, cubed
1 tablespoon soy sauce
4 oz (125 g) spinach, washed, tough stems discarded, and leaves coarsely chopped
1/4 teaspoon ground white pepper

1 Bring the stock to a boil in a pot. Add the tofu and soy sauce and simmer for 2 minutes.
2 Add the spinach, cook for 2 minutes, then season with pepper and serve.

Serves 4
Preparation time: 5 mins
Cooking time: 10 mins

Clockwise from top: Egg Drop Soup, Tofu and Spinach Soup, and Corn and Mushroom Soup (recipe not given).

Classic Hot and Sour Soup

4 cups (1 liter) vegetable stock or Chinese Chicken Stock (page 8)
1 teaspoon salt
1 teaspoon sugar
$1/_2$ tablespoon grated ginger
$1/_2$ cup (60 g) fresh or frozen green peas
1 large tomato, diced
1 cake soft tofu (10 oz/ 300 g), diced
5 dried black Chinese mushrooms, soaked in warm water for 20 minutes, tough stems discarded and caps diced
2 tablespoons soy sauce
2 tablespoons black Chinese vinegar
1 teaspoon sesame oil
$1/_2$ teaspoon ground black pepper
$1/_2$ teaspoon ground Sichuan pepper or *sansho* pepper
2 eggs, beaten
2 tablespoons cornstarch dissolved in 2 tablespoons water
3 green onions (scallions), sliced
Pinch of ground white pepper
Chili oil, to serve (optional, see note)
Black Chinese vinegar, to serve (optional)

1 Bring the stock to a boil in a large pot. Add the salt, sugar, ginger, peas, tomato, tofu and mushrooms. Return to a boil, reduce the heat and simmer for 3 more minutes.

2 Add the soy sauce, black Chinese vinegar, sesame oil, black pepper and ground Sichuan pepper. Stir to mix well. Slowly drizzle the beaten egg into the soup and let sit for 1 minute. Do not stir.

3 Stir the cornstarch mixture, then pour it slowly into the simmering soup while stirring gently. Keep stirring until the soup thickens. Simmer for 1 more minute, then turn off the heat.

4 Serve hot, garnished with green onions and white pepper. Add a few drops of chili oil and black Chinese vinegar, if desired.

Chili oil is made from dried chilies or ground red pepper steeped in oil. Bottled chili oil is available in Asian markets, or you can make your own. Heat $3/_4$ cup (190 ml) of oil in a wok or skillet and add 1 tablespoon of Sichuan peppercorns and 2 dried chilies (deseeded and sliced). Cook over low heat for 10 minutes, then cool and store in a glass container for 2–3 days. Strain and discard the peppercorns and chilies. Store in an airtight glass jar and keep in a cool place for up to 6 months.

Serves 4
Preparation time: 30 mins
Cooking time: 10 mins

Chinese Cabbage Soup

10 oz (300 g) *bok choy* or Chinese (Napa) cabbage, cut in half lengthwise

3 dried black Chinese mushrooms, soaked in warm water for 20 minutes, then drained

2 cups (500 ml) Chinese Chicken Stock (page 8) or canned chicken stock

2 tablespoons sliced ham

$^1/_2$ cup (60 g) dried shrimp, soaked in warm water, drained

$^1/_2$ teaspoon salt, or to taste

1 Bring a pot of water to a boil and briefly blanch the vegetables. Drain and chopped into $1^1/_4$-in (3-cm) pieces. Halve the mushroom caps if they are large and discard the tough stems.

2 Bring the Chinese Chicken Stock to a boil in a stockpot. Add the ham, mushrooms, dried shrimp, vegetables and salt.

3 Bring the stock back to a boil and skim off any foam from the surface. Reduce the heat and simmer until the vegetables are very tender.

4 Remove from the heat and pour into a soup tureen and serve immediately.

Serves 2–3
Preparation time: 20 mins
Cooking time: 1 hour

Simple Noodle Soup

1 tablespoon oil
1 slice fresh ginger
$^1/_2$ teaspoon rice wine
$2^1/_2$ cups (625 ml)
  Chinese Chicken Stock
  (page 8) or canned
  chicken stock
2 tablespoons minced
  ham or bacon
10 oz (300 g) fresh
  noodles or 180 g
  (6 oz) dried noodle,
  blanched in hot water,
  then drained
$3^1/_2$ oz (100 g) green
  vegetables such as
  bok choy

1 In a large saucepan, heat the oil and stir-fry the ginger until pungent then discard the ginger.
2 Pour in the rice wine, let it sizzle, then add the Chinese Chicken Stock and minced ham. Bring to a boil, add the noodles and simmer for 1 minute to allow the noodles to heat through. Remove the noodles and divide into individual bowls.
3 Blanch the vegetables in the remaining stock, then remove and arrange in the bowl with the noodles. Pour the hot stock over the noodles and serve.

Serves 2–3
Preparation time: 15 mins
Cooking time: 10 mins

Hot and Spicy Sichuan Noodles

It's hard to think of any time of the day when noodles are not popular in China; they're eaten for breakfast, as a mid-morning snack, for lunch, as something to keep you going until dinner, and as a late-night restorative. This spicy Sichuan favorite is often sold at street-side stalls and by mobile vendors, known as hawk-

$1/_2$ tablespoon Sichuan peppercorns or *sansho* pepper

$1^1/_2$ tablespoons peanut oil

1 teaspoon oil

$1^1/_4$ cups (250 g) ground pork

2 cups (500 ml) Chinese Chicken Stock (page 8) or canned chicken stock

$1/_2$ cup (125 g) preserved salted radish (*chye poh,* see note), diced

4 tablespoons soy sauce

$1^1/_2$ tablespoons black Chinese vinegar

1 tablespoon minced garlic

2 teaspoons sesame oil

1 teaspoon chili oil

$1/_4$ teaspoon ground white pepper

1 lb (500 g) fresh wheat noodles or 8 oz (250g) dried wheat noodles

4 green onions (scallions), finely sliced, to garnish

1 Heat a wok over low heat and dry-fry the Sichuan peppercorns or *sansho* pepper for 2–3 minutes until fragrant. Add the peanut oil and cook over low heat for 10 minutes to infuse it with the flavor of the peppercorns. Cool, then strain the oil, discarding the peppercorns. Set aside.

2 Heat the oil in a wok over high heat and stir-fry the pork for 2–3 minutes, or until cooked. Set aside.

3 Combine the Sichuan peppercorn oil, Chinese Chicken Stock, preserved salted radish, soy sauce, black Chinese vinegar, garlic, sesame oil, chili oil and white pepper in a saucepan. Keep warm over medium heat.

4 Bring a pot of water to a boil and cook the noodles. Fresh noodles will take about 2 minutes to cook, dried noodles about 4 minutes. Drain the noodles and divide into 4 individual bowls.

5 Bring the warm stock to a boil. Remove from the heat and pour into the bowls over the noodles. Top with the pork and garnish with sliced green onions. Serve immediately.

Preserved salted radish or *chye poh* is pickled Japanese radish or daikon. Often added to dishes for its crunchy texture and salty flavor, it keeps almost indefinitely and is available at Asian markets. The Japanese version may be substituted.

Serves 4
Preparation time: **20 mins**
Cooking time: **15 mins**

Chicken Chow Mein

1 boneless, skinless chicken breast, thinly sliced
4 tablespoons oil
7 oz (200 g) dried egg noodles, soaked in warm water until soft, then drained
1$1/_2$ cups (75 g) bean sprouts, cleaned
2 green onions (scallions), cut into lengths

Marinade
1 teaspoon ginger juice (see note)
1 teaspoon rice wine
1 teaspoon soy sauce
1 teaspoon cornstarch
2 tablespoons water
$1/_4$ teaspoon pepper
1 teaspoon sesame oil

Seasonings
$1/_2$ cup (125 ml) warm chicken stock
1 teaspoon rice wine
1 tablespoon soy sauce
2 teaspoons oyster sauce
1 teaspoon sugar

1 Combine all the Marinade ingredients in a bowl. Add the sliced chicken and set aside to marinate for 15 minutes.
2 Combine the Seasonings in a small bowl and set aside.
3 Heat 3 tablespoons of the oil in a wok until hot, then add the noodles. Fry very quickly until the noodles are golden brown and crisp, about 1 minute. Remove the noodles from the wok and place onto a platter.
4 Add the remaining 1 tablespoon of oil to the wok and stir-fry the chicken vigorously over high heat until cooked, about 1 minute. Add the Seasonings, the bean sprouts and green onion, and continue to stir-fry vigorously for another 30 seconds, until the sauce thickens. Quickly turn off the heat and pour the chicken mixture and sauce over the noodles. Serve hot.

To make the **ginger juice,** grate 4 in (10 cm) young ginger to make $1/_2$ cup of grated ginger. Mix with 2 tablespoons water, then strain the mixture through a fine sieve, pressing with the back of a spoon, to obtain $1/_4$ cup (60 ml) of ginger juice.

Serves 2–3
Preparation time: 30 mins
Cooking time: 20 mins

Noodle Salad with Ham and Vegetables

1 lb (500 g) cooked noodles (Japanese ramen, soba or Chinese egg noodles)
1 tablespoon garlic oil, at room temperature
2 tablespoons olive oil
1 small shallot, peeled and smashed
1 cup (50 g) bean sprouts
$1/4$ cup (30 g) dried shrimp, soaked and ground in a blender
1 cup (100 g) carrots, cut into matchsticks
1 red finger-length chili, deseeded and thinly sliced
$1/2$ cup (125 g) ham, cut into thin strips
1 cup (100 g) cucumber, peeled and deseeded, cut into thin strips

Seasonings

3 tablespoons sesame paste or peanut butter
1–2 tablespoons sugar
3 tablespoons soy sauce
4 tablespoons chicken stock
1 teaspoon chili oil
1 teaspoon sesame oil
$1/4$ teaspoon freshly ground pepper

1 Wash the cooked noodles, drain and coat with the garlic oil.
2 Heat 1 tablespoon of the olive oil in a wok and stir-fry the shallot, then discard the shallot (it is used only to impart flavor to the oil). Add the bean sprouts and stir-fry for a few seconds, then remove and set aside.
3 Reheat the wok with the remaining oil and stir-fry the ground dried shrimp. Add the carrots and chili, stir well. Return the bean sprouts to the wok together with the ham, cucumber and noodles. Toss to mix well. Remove from the heat and, transfer to a dish and refrigerate until cold.
4 To serve, stir the Seasonings together in a bowl. Adjust the flavor to taste and pour over the noodles. Serve cold.

Serves 4
Preparation time: 20 mins
Cooking time: 20 mins

Black Bean Sauce Noodles

This is a quick and simple noodle dish which makes an excellent one-dish lunch or part of a multi-course dinner. It may be served warm—straight from the pot, or it can be prepared in advance and served at room temperature.

1 lb (500 g) fresh wheat noodles (not egg noodles) or 8 oz/250 g dried wheat noodles
1 tablespoon sesame oil
3 tablespoons oil
2 tablespoons fermented black bean sauce (see note)
2 tablespoons water
1 large carrot, peeled and thinly sliced
1 cake (about 10 oz/300 g) pressed tofu (*taukwa*), sliced into fine strips
3 florets fresh black wood ear fungus, finely sliced
25 fresh snow peas, ends snapped off and strings removed, or 1 cup (150 g) fresh or frozen green peas
3 cloves garlic, finely sliced
1 teaspoon sugar
1 teaspoon rice vinegar

Serves 4–6
Preparation time: 30 mins
Cooking time: 20 mins

1 Bring a large pot of water to a boil, blanch the noodles briefly to revive them. If using dried noodles, follow the instructions or cook them for 3–4 minutes until the noodles are tender. Drain, rinse in cold water and transfer to a colander to drain well. Place the drained noodles in a large bowl, add the sesame oil and toss well.

2 Heat the oil in a wok or skillet till hot but not smoking, add the fermented black bean sauce, stir-fry quickly, then add the water and stir to mix. Add the carrots, pressed tofu strips, black fungus and snow peas or green peas. Stir-fry for 3 minutes, then add the rest of the ingredients and continue to stir-fry for another 3–5 minutes. Transfer all the cooked ingredients and sauce into the bowl of noodles. Toss to mix well. Serve in a large bowl or divide into individual serving bowls.

Fermented black bean sauce is a richly-flavored seasoning made from fermented black beans (also called salted black beans)—soybeans that have been fermented and preserved in salt, hence their strong, salty flavor. Mainly used to season a number of dishes, especially fish, beef and chicken. It is sold in jars and can be found in the ethnic or international section of many supermarkets.

Chopped **fresh coriander leaves (cilantro)** may be added as a garnish.

Fried *Hor Fun* Noodles

¹/₄ cup (50 g) bacon or belly pork, diced
2 tablespoons water
3 cloves garlic, minced
1 teaspoon bottled chili sauce
¹/₂ cup (100 g) sliced pork
¹/₃ cup (100 g) peeled fresh shrimp
¹/₂ cup (100 g) sliced fresh squid
1 teaspoon soy sauce
1 tablespoon dark soy sauce
1 teaspoon oyster sauce
¹/₄ teaspoon salt
¹/₂ teaspoon pepper
2 cups (100 g) bean sprouts
1 lb (500 g) fresh *kway teow* or *hor fun* noodles or 8 oz (250 g) dried *hor fun* or river noodles, scalded in boiling water, rinsed and drained
1 red finger-length chili, deseeded and sliced
Sprigs of fresh coriander leaves (cilantro), to garnish

1 Cook the bacon or belly pork in the water to render the fat, until it turns crisp. Remove and drain on paper towels. Leave 2 tablespoons of the oil in the wok. Discard the rest.
2 Heat the oil and stir-fry the garlic and chili over low-medium heat for about 30 seconds. Increase the heat, add the pork and stir-fry for 2 minutes. Add the shrimp and squid and stir-fry for another 2 minutes. Season with the soy sauce, oyster sauce, salt and pepper.
3 Add the bean sprouts and stir-fry for 2 minutes, then put in the noodles and stir-fry until well mixed and heated through. Stir in the crisp bacon bits and transfer to a serving dish. Garnish with chili and coriander leaves.

For a healthier alternative, use 3 tablespoons oil instead of the pork fat to fry the ingredients.

Serves 4
Preparation time: **15 mins**   Cooking time: **10–15 mins**

Egg Noodles with Mushrooms

5 oz (150 g) dried egg noodles
1 tablespoon oil
1 clove garlic, bruised
3–4 large fresh shiitake mushrooms, thinly sliced
1 cup (90 g) thinly sliced button mushrooms
$1/2$ cup (125 ml) chicken stock or water
2 teaspoons soy sauce
2 tablespoons oyster sauce
1 teaspoon sugar
$1/4$ teaspoon pepper
1 teaspoon sesame oil

Serves 2
Preparation time: **30 mins**
Cooking time: **20 mins**

1 Bring a pot of water to a boil and blanch the noodles for about 30 seconds. Rinse them with cold water and drain in a colander.

2 Heat the oil in a wok and stir-fry the garlic until aromatic, then discard the garlic. Add the mushrooms to the wok and stir-fry for 20 seconds. Mix in the noodles, and combine.

3 Pour in the stock, soy sauce, oyster sauce, sugar and pepper. Simmer until the noodles have absorbed all the stock. Sprinkle in the sesame oil and toss thoroughly. If the mushrooms fall to the bottom when you dish out the noodles, arrange them on top of the noodles.

Both fresh or dried Chinese egg noodles can be used for this recipe. If egg noodles are not available, substitute wheat noodles.

Steamed Rice with Chinese Sausages

1¹/₂ cups (300 g) un-
cooked rice
1 teaspoon salt
1 tablespoon oil
2 cups (500 ml) water
3 dried sweet Chinese
sausages, rinsed and
patted dry
1 green onion (scallion),
very thinly sliced

Seasonings
1 tablespoon soy sauce
1 tablespoon dark soy
sauce
1 tablespoon sugar
¹/₄ teaspoon pepper

1 Wash the rice thoroughly. Leave it to soak in clean water for 20 minutes. Drain and place the rice into a claypot or medium pot. Stir in the salt and oil and mix well. Pour in the the water.

2 Arrange the pork sausages on top of the rice, cover and simmer over low heat, about 10 minutes. Stir the rice once and continue to simmer for another 3 minutes, then cook over very low heat for another 15–20 minutes. Turn off the heat and set aside for 10–15 minutes.

3 Meanwhile, combine the Seasonings in a small bowl. Remove the sausages and slice them thinly at an angle. Arrange the sliced sausages on the rice, pour the Seasonings over the sausages and rice. Sprinkle the green onion on top and serve hot.

Serves 2
Preparation time: **25 mins**
Cooking time: **45 mins**

Claypot Chicken Rice

Traditionally, this dish is cooked and served in a claypot. If you do not have a claypot, cooking the dish in a saucepan or rice cooker will produce similar results.

1 lb (500 g) boneless
  chicken thighs, skinned
1 tablespoon ginger juice
  (page 32)
1 tablespoon soy sauce
1 tablespoon dark soy
  sauce
1 tablespoon oyster sauce
2 teaspoons sesame oil
1 teaspoon salt
$^1/_2$ teaspoon pepper
1 tablespoon sugar
2 cups (400 g) uncooked
  rice
2$^1/_4$ cups (560 ml) water
10 fresh or dried chest-
  nuts, boiled until just
  soft, cut in half
2 dried sweet Chinese
  sausages (*lap cheong*),
  thinly sliced
2 tablespoons oil

Garnishes
3 tablespoons Crispy Fried
  Shallots (page 9)
1 green onion (scallion),
  thinly sliced, to garnish
Seasoned Sliced Chilies
  (page 9), to serve

1 Place the chicken in a large bowl. Combine the ginger juice, soy sauces, oyster sauce, sesame oil, salt, pepper and sugar, and rub into the chicken. Set aside for 20–30 minutes to marinate.

2 Wash the rice thoroughly and drain. Place the rice and water in a claypot and bring to a boil. Then reduce the heat and simmer, covered, for 15 minutes until most of the water has been absorbed.

3 Place the marinated chicken, boiled chestnuts and dried sweet Chinese sausages on top of the rice and drizzle 2 tablespoons of cooking oil in. Cover the claypot with a tight-fitting lid and cook on low heat, undisturbed, for 20 minutes.

4 Flake the rice with a fork, cover, and allow the rice to cook for another 15 minutes. Garnish with the Crispy Fried Shallots, green onion and serve with a small bowl of Seasoned Sliced Chilies on the side.

Serves 4
Preparation time: 30 mins
Cooking time: 50 mins

Classic Fried Rice

4 cups (400 g) cooked
  rice, chilled in the fridge
3 teaspoons oil
2 eggs, lightly beaten
8 fresh shrimp, peeled,
  deveined, and diced
$^1/_4$ cup (50 g) thinly
  sliced chicken or pork
2 dried sweet Chinese
  sausages (*lap cheong*),
  thinly sliced diagonally
2 green onions (scal-
  lions), thinly sliced
$^1/_2$ cup (50 g) sliced
  asparagus or green peas
$^1/_4$ teaspoon salt
1 portion Hunan Chili
  Relish (page 8)

1 Break up the rice grains with a fork and set aside.
2 Heat 1 teaspoon of oil in a wok. Cook the beaten
eggs until set. Break the omelet into small pieces with
a spatula. Remove from the wok and set aside.
3 Heat the remaining oil over high heat in the wok
and stir-fry the remaining ingredients, except the rice
and salt, for 2 minutes. Add the rice and salt and stir-
fry for another 4–5 minutes, turning constantly to
brown the rice. Add the omelet pieces, stir well to
combine. Remove from the heat and serve with the
Hunan Chili Relish (page 8).

If you don't have Chinese sausages, any kind of sausage,
ham or bacon can be substituted.

Serves 4
Preparation time: **5 mins**
Cooking time: **5 mins**

Fried Rice with Ground Beef and Lettuce

³/₄ cup (150 g) ground
beef
2 tablespoons oil
1 egg, beaten
3 cups (300 g) cooked rice
1 tablespoon soy sauce
¹/₂ teaspoon pepper
1 cup (100 g) sliced lettuce
1 teaspoon thinly sliced
green onions (scallions)
1 teaspoon sesame oil

Marinade
2 teaspoons soy sauce
1 teaspoon sugar
1 teaspoon rice wine
1 teaspoon cornstarch
¹/₄ cup (60 ml) water

1 Combine all the Marinade ingredients in a bowl.
Add the beef, stir well, and set aside to marinate for
10 minutes.
2 Heat 1 tablespoon of the oil in a wok and fry the
ground beef until just browned, breaking it up with a
spatula as it cooks. Remove from the pan and set
aside.
3 Clean and dry the wok, then heat the remaining oil
and scramble the egg for 20 seconds. Stir in the
cooked rice and stir-fry well.
4 Add the soy sauce and pepper, ground beef and lettuce. Stir-fry to combine evenly. Add the sliced green
onion and sesame oil. Transfer to a serving dish and
serve hot.

Serves 2
Preparation time: 20 mins
Cooking time: 20 mins

Sichuan Chicken

This is a style of chicken native to Chengdu, the provincial capital of Sichuan. Like so many Sichuan dishes, the chicken here is cooked twice, first by deep-frying, then by braising with seasonings. The braising stage of the process removes much of the oil that clings to the chicken after deep-frying, thereby making the dish far less heavy and far more easy to digest, while still retaining the crisp texture imparted by the initial frying.

3 boneless chicken thighs, (about 12 oz/350 g)
1^1/$_2$ cups (375 ml) oil, for deep-frying
3 tablespoons oil, for stir-frying
3 cloves garlic, finely chopped
5 slices fresh ginger, finely chopped
10 Sichuan peppercorns
1^1/$_2$ cups (375 ml) water
2 stalks fresh celery, strings removed, diced

Sauce

1 tablespoon black bean paste
1 teaspoon sugar
2 teaspoons rice wine
2 teaspoons sesame oil
2 teaspoons cornstarch mixed with 2 tablespoons water

Serves 4
Preparation time: 20 mins
Cooking time: 5 mins

1 Cut the chicken thighs into chunks. Heat 1^1/$_2$ cups (375 ml) of oil until hot, then add the chicken chunks and deep-fry until golden. Remove from the oil and drain on a wire rack or paper towels.

2 Combine the Sauce ingredients together in a bowl and set aside.

3 Heat 3 tablespoons of oil until hot, but not smoking. Add the garlic, ginger and Sichuan peppercorns, and stir-fry swiftly to release the aromas, about 30 seconds.

4 Add the chicken to the oil, stir-fry for 1 minute, then add the Sauce. Stir to blend all flavors. Add the water and stir until it returns to a boil. Reduce the heat to medium, cover, and braise slowly until most of the liquid has evaporated, leaving the chicken bubbling in a thick sauce.

5 Transfer to a serving dish, sprinkle the celery evenly over the top, and serve.

You may also try this recipe with fresh fish, preferably fish such as tuna, swordfish, marlin, etc. Prepare the fish in the same way as chicken, but reduce the cooking time a little. Chopped green onions and/or chopped fresh coriander leaves (cilantro) also go very well as a garnish for this recipe.

Black Bean Sauce Chicken

Tender chicken and crisp snow peas simmered in a flavorful, salty black bean sauce.

2 boneless skinless chicken breasts (about 1 lb/500 g), cut into strips
$1/2$ tablespoon grated ginger
$1/2$ tablespoon cornstarch, blended with 1 tablespoon rice wine or sake
2 tablespoons oil
4 small shallots, diced
1 clove garlic, minced
2 tablespoons bottled black bean and garlic sauce, or $1/3$ cup (20 g) whole salted black beans, soaked and mashed
$1/2$ cup (125 ml) chicken stock
$1 1/2$ teaspoons sugar
2 green onions (scallions), cut into sections

1 Combine the chicken strips with the ginger and cornstarch mixture in a bowl, and leave to marinate for 10 minutes.

2 Heat the oil in a wok over medium-high heat. When the oil is hot, add the shallots and garlic, and stir-fry for 30 seconds. Add the black bean and garlic sauce (or salted black beans) and stir-fry for another 30 seconds.

3 Add the chicken, chicken stock and sugar, and bring to a boil. Reduce the heat to low and simmer for 3 minutes. Add the green onions and stir-fry to mix well. Remove from the heat and transfer to a serving dish.

If using whole salted black beans, soak the beans in enough hot water to cover for 30 minutes. Rinse, drain, then roughly mash the beans.

Serves 4
Preparation time: 20 mins + 10 mins marinating time
Cooking time: 10 mins

Chili Chicken with Peanuts

Chili and chicken is one of the all-time great culinary combinations, and virtually every Asian culture has various versions of this dynamic duo. In Sichuan cuisine, there are at least a dozen major variations on this theme. This one is for those whose palates enjoy a potent pungency in their food. For a hotter taste, keep the chili seeds and fibers; for milder taste, remove them first.

3 boneless chicken thighs (about 12 oz/350 g)
2 tablespoons oil
8 cloves garlic, finely chopped
2–3 red finger-length chilies, finely chopped
1/2 cup (50 g) unsalted roasted peanuts
2 green onions (scallions), cut into sections

Marinade
1 teaspoon soy sauce
1/2 teaspoon cornstarch
1 teaspoon rice wine

Sauce
2 tablespoons bottled hot bean paste
1 teaspoon sugar, or more to taste
1 teaspoon soy sauce
1/2 teaspoon rice vinegar
2 teaspoons sesame oil
1 teaspoon cornstarch mixed with 1/2 cup (125 ml) water

1 Cut the chicken into chunks.

2 Combine the Marinade ingredients in a bowl and add the chicken chunks. Set aside to marinate for about 15 minutes.

3 Combine all the Sauce ingredients in a bowl and set aside.

4 Heat the oil in a wok until hot. Add the chopped garlic and chili and stir-fry quickly for 30 seconds, then add the marinated chicken and continue to stir-fry until the meat turns color and becomes firm, about 3–4 minutes. Add the peanuts and green onion and stir-fry to mix well.

5 Stir the Sauce again to mix the ingredients, then pour over the chicken and stir to coat well. Cover, reduce the heat to medium, and simmer for about 3 minutes. Transfer to a serving dish.

Fresh or frozen green peas add color and flavor to this dish, and may be added along with, or instead of, the peanuts. Either chopped fresh coriander leaves (cilantro), or chopped parsley, may be added as a garnish.

Serves 4
Preparation time: **20 mins**
Cooking time: **10 mins**

Fragrant Crispy Duck

Duck is an excellent dish for the autumn and winter, and is renowned for its restorative benefits to the kidneys, a primary source of human vitality. This distinctive method of preparation, which involves steaming a whole duck first, then frying it, seals in the duck's essential flavors and nutrients and produces a delicious crispy skin on the outside.

2 teaspoons salt
2 teaspoons Sichuan
  peppercorns
1 teaspoon black
  peppercorns
4 green onions (scallions), finely sliced
3 slices fresh ginger,
  finely chopped
1 tablespoon rice wine
1 whole duck (about
  4 lbs/2 kgs), cleaned
6 star anise pods
Fresh coriander leaves
  (cilantro), to garnish

Serves 4
Preparation time: 10 mins
Cooking time: 10 mins

1 Heat a dry wok over medium flame. Add the salt, Sichuan and black peppercorns, and dry-roast them continuously for 1–2 minutes, until the peppercorns are fragrant. Grind to a coarse powder in a blender.
2 Mix the ground salt and pepper powder with the green onions, ginger and rice wine in a bowl until well combined. Rub this mixture all over the duck, inside and outside. Place the star anise and any remaining mixture inside the duck's abdominal cavity. Place the duck on a dish, cover with cellophane wrap, and put in the fridge to marinate for 2–3 hours.
3 Set a steaming rack over a pot or wok large enough to hold the duck. Bring water to a boil in the pot, then place the duck in a heat-proof dish and set it on the rack in the steamer. Cover tightly, and steam the duck for $1^1/_2$ hours, making sure to replenish the water from time to time as it evaporates.
4 Remove the duck and leave aside on a rack to cool.
5 Pour enough oil into a large wok to fill it about $^1/_3$ full (about $1^1/_2$–2 liters/6–8 cups). Heat until smoking hot, then reduce the heat slightly and very carefully immerse the whole duck into the hot oil, breast side down, covering the duck completely in oil if possible. Deep-fry for 3–4 minutes, until the skin turns a rich golden brown. If the duck is not fully immersed in the oil, turn and fry the other side for 2 more minutes. Remove the duck from the oil and drain it on a rack.
6 Once the duck has cooled, place it on a chopping board, cut it in half and separate the legs and wings. Using a Chinese cleaver, chop it into chunks. Arrange the duck on a platter and garnish with fresh coriander leaves.

Diced Chicken with Dried Chilies

2 chicken breasts
1 teaspoon sugar
1 teaspoon soy sauce
1 teaspoon black Chinese vinegar
1 teaspoon rice wine
1 teaspoon cornstarch
$1/_3$ cup (80 ml) water
3 tablespoons oil
8–10 dried chilies, deseeded and sliced
$1/_2$ teaspoon ground star anise or Sichuan pepper
$1/_2$ teaspoon black pepper
1 teaspoon minced garlic
1 teaspoon minced ginger
2 green onions (scallions) cut into lengths
$1/_4$ teaspoon sesame oil

1 Debone the chicken breasts and cut into chunks.
2 Combine the sugar, soy sauce, vinegar, rice wine, cornstarch and water in a small bowl. Set aside.
3 Heat the oil in a wok until very hot. Stir-fry the chicken until golden brown, about 2 minutes. Remove and drain on paper towels. Discard all but 1 tablespoon of the oil.
4 Heat the reserved oil and stir-fry the chilies until they turn color and begin to smoke, about 2–3 minutes. Remove the chilies from the wok and set aside. Then add the ground spices, garlic and ginger to the wok and stir-fry for 1 minute until fragrant. Add the sauce mixture and green onions. Stir-fry for 30 seconds, then return the chicken and chilies to the wok and fry for 1 more minute until the sauce thickens. Drizzle in the sesame oil. Remove from the heat and serve immediately.

Serves 4
Preparation time: 10 mins
Cooking time: 20 mins

Black Soy Pork

1 1/4 lbs (600 g) belly
pork, skin left on
3 tablespoons dark soy
sauce
3 tablespoons soy sauce
2 teaspoons sugar
1/4 teaspoon pepper
10 small shallots, peeled
4 cloves garlic
1 tablespoon oil
1 tablespoon black bean
paste
8 dried black Chinese
mushrooms, soaked to
soften, stems discarded
4 cups (1 liter) water
One 5-oz (150-g) can
bamboo shoots, drained
and cut into wedges

1 Cut the pork into bite-sized chunks. Season with the soy sauces, sugar and pepper. Set aside to marinate for 30 minutes, then drain, reserving the marinade.

2 Grind the shallots and garlic in a blender until fine. Heat the oil in a wok and stir-fry the ground mixture over medium heat for 2 minutes. Add the black bean paste and stir-fry for 30 seconds. Add the mushrooms and stir-fry for 1 minute.

3 Add the meat to the wok and stir-fry until it changes color, 3–4 minutes. Add the water and reserved marinade and bring to a boil. Reduce the heat, cover and simmer until the meat is just tender, about 45 minutes.

4 Add the bamboo shoots. Cover and simmer, stirring occasionally, until the meat is very soft and the sauce thickens, 15–20 minutes. Serve hot with steamed rice.

Serves 4–6
Preparation time: 15 mins + 30 mins marinating time
Cooking time: 1 hour 10 mins

Twice-cooked Pork

In this recipe, the pork is first pre-cooked in boiling water to render out some of the fat. It is then finely sliced and stir-fried with Sichuan seasonings. The distinctive taste of this dish is created primarily by two ingredients: black bean paste and hoisin sauce. The former is highly aromatic while the latter is sweet and salty.

1 lb (500 g) fresh belly pork or pork loin
2–3 leeks, washed
2 tablespoons oil
6 thin slices fresh ginger
1 green and 1 red bell pepper, cored and cut into squares
1 red finger-length chili, deseeded and sliced

Sauce
1 tablespoon black bean paste
2 teaspoons hoisin sauce
2 teaspoons sugar
2 teaspoons rice wine
1 tablespoon soy sauce
1 tablespoon water

Serves 4
Preparation time: 30 mins
Cooking time: 10 min

1 Bring a pot of water to a rolling boil. Add the pork, let the water return to a boil, reduce the heat to medium, simmer, and boil until thoroughly cooked, about 25 minutes. Remove the pork and when cooled, cut the it across the grain into wafer-thin slices. If using belly pork, slice it so that there is a strip of fat in each piece.
2 Wash the leeks well, cut off and discard the tops of the green leaves, keeping just the white stalks and the tender portions of the leaves. Cut each stalk in half lengthwise, and then slice it into sections.
3 Combine the Sauce ingredients in a bowl and set aside.
4 Heat 1 tablespoon of the oil in a wok until hot. Add the ginger, bell pepper and chili, and stir-fry swiftly for 1 minute, then add the leeks and continue stir-frying for 1 more minute. Remove and set aside on a plate.
5 Add the remaining oil to the wok, and when hot, fry the sliced pork quickly for 1–2 minutes, until the pork is seared around the edges.
6 Return the fried leeks mixture to the wok. Stir to mix well, then immediately pour in the Sauce. Stir to blend, and simmer for about 3 minutes over medium heat. Transfer to a platter and serve with steamed rice.

Pork with Green Peppers and Peanuts

4 oz (125 g) boneless
  pork loin or shoulder
6 egg whites
3 tablespoons cornstarch
3 tablespoons oil
2 green bell peppers,
  deseeded and sliced
3 tablespoons roasted
  unsalted peanuts, skins
  removed
1/4 teaspoon chili oil
  (see note)

Sauce
1 tablespoon cornstarch
3 tablespoons chicken
  stock or water
1 tablespoon rice wine
1 tablespoon soy sauce
1 teaspoon salt, or to
  taste
1 green onion (scallion),
  finely chopped
1 tablespoon minced
  ginger
2 cloves garlic, minced
1 1/2 teaspoons sugar

Serves 4
Preparation time: **15 mins**
Cooking time: **10 mins**

1 Prepare the Sauce by first dissolving the cornstarch in the stock or water in a bowl. Add the rest of the ingredients, and stir until the sugar completely dissolves. Set aside.

2 Wash the pork and cut into small cubes.

3 Beat the egg whites and stir in the cornstarch. Add the pork cubes and mix well to coat. Set aside.

4 Heat the oil in a wok over medium-high heat. Add the pork cubes and stir-fry for about 1 minute, cooking them just long enough to seal in the juices. Turn off the heat and transfer the pork cubes to a plate, reserving the oil in the wok.

5 Reheat the reserved oil in the wok over high heat. Add the bell pepper cubes and stir-fry for about 1 minute. Return the pork cubes to the wok. Stir the Sauce in the bowl to blend the ingredients, then add it to the wok.

6 Add the peanuts and chili oil. Bring the contents to a boil and continue to stir-fry until the Sauce thickens. Remove from the heat, transfer to a serving platter and serve immediately.

Chili oil is made from dried chilies or ground red pepper steeped in oil. Bottled chili oil is available in Asian markets, or you can make your own. Heat 3/4 cup (190 ml) of oil in a wok or skillet and add 1 tablespoon of Sichuan peppercorns and 2 dried chilies (deseeded and sliced). Cook over low heat for 10 minutes, then cool and store in a glass container for 2–3 days. Strain and discard the peppercorns and chilies. Store in an airtight glass jar and keep in a cool place for up to 6 months.

Five Spice Spareribs

1 1/2 lbs (700 g) pork
  spareribs
4 tablespoons soy sauce
2 tablespoons sugar
Oil, for deep-frying
2 green onions (scal-
  lions), chopped
2 thick slices fresh ginger,
  minced
1 teaspoon rice wine
1/2 teaspoon fennel seeds
1 teaspoon brown sugar
5 teaspoons rice vinegar
1 teaspoon salt, or to
  taste

Serves 4
Preparation time: 15 mins
Cooking time: 10 mins

1 Wash the spareribs and chop into short pieces using a meat cleaver. Cover with cold water and soak for 5 minutes. Remove, drain and marinate in 2 tablespoons of the soy sauce for 15 minutes. Drain, dry well and rub with the sugar. Set aside.

2 Heat the oil in a wok over high heat. Add the spareribs and deep-fry until golden brown. Remove and set aside. Pour out the oil, leaving just enough oil to cover the bottom of the wok.

3 Reheat the wok and add the green onions and ginger. Return the spareribs to the wok. Stir in the rice wine, fennel seeds, brown sugar, vinegar, salt and the remaining soy sauce. Stir-fry for about 1 minute. Reduce the heat to low and simmer until the sauce thickens and the meat falls from the bones. Remove and serve hot.

Sweet Soy Pork Ribs

2 lbs (1 kg) meaty pork ribs
2 tablespoons oil
2 teaspoons minced garlic
1 tablespoon minced ginger
3 tablespoons fermented bean curd or fermented black beans, mashed
2 teaspoons sugar
2 tablespoons dark soy sauce
1 tablespoon rice wine
3 cups (750 ml) water
1 teaspoon pepper

Marinade
2 tablespoons rice wine
2 tablespoons sesame oil
1 tablespoon soy sauce
1 tablespoon cornstarch

1 Chop the pork ribs into chunks and place them into a large bowl with the Marinade ingredients. Mix well. Set aside for 10 minutes.

2 Heat the oil in a wok until very hot, and stir-fry the pork ribs over high heat until the ribs turn light brown, 2–3 minutes. Lower the heat, add the garlic and ginger and stir-fry for a few seconds. Add the fermented bean curd or black beans and sugar. Stir-fry for 1 more minute. Add the soy sauce and rice wine, and combine well. Pour in the water and bring to a boil.

3 Lower the heat, cover and simmer until the meat is tender, 50–60 minutes, stirring several times so the ribs cook evenly. Add more water if the sauce dries up before the meat is done. Remove from the heat, season with pepper and transfer to a serving dish. Serve with plain rice.

Serves 4–6
Preparation time: 10 mins + 10 mins marinating
Cooking time: 50 mins

Sweet and Sour Spareribs

The sauce should be bright and translucent, the meat tender and succulent, and the flavor neither too sweet nor too sour, so you should taste and adjust the seasonings depending on the type of vinegar used. If you prefer, you can use a boneless cut of pork such as loin instead of spareribs.

1 1/2 lbs (700g) pork spareribs or 1 lb (500 g) boneless pork loin
1 egg yolk, beaten
1 tablespoon cornstarch
1 teaspoon water
Oil, for deep-frying

Marinade
1/2 teaspoon salt
1/2 teaspoon ground black pepper
1 1/2 teaspoons sugar
1 tablespoon brandy

Sauce
1 tablespoon oil
1 green bell pepper, cored and sliced into thin strips
3 tablespoons sugar
2 tablespoons rice vinegar
1 tablespoon soy sauce
1 tablespoon bottled tomato ketchup
1/2 teaspoon sesame oil
4 tablespoons chicken stock or water
2 teaspoons cornstarch dissolved in 1 tablespoon water

1 Wash and chop the spareribs into chunks.
2 Combine the Marinade ingredients in a big bowl and stir until the sugar completely dissolves. Add the spareribs and mix well. Set aside in the refrigerator to marinate for at least 30 minutes. Turn the spareribs to allow the Marinade to penetrate.
3 Combine the egg yolk with the cornstarch and add enough water to make a thin batter. Remove the spareribs from the Marinade and coat them with the batter.
4 Heat the oil in a wok until very hot and fry the spareribs in batches, until they turn crisp and golden brown, about 3 minutes. Remove and drain on paper towels. Set aside and keep warm in the oven set to low heat. Pour out the oil and discard.
5 Make the Sauce by heating the oil in a wok until hot, then add the green bell pepper strips and stir-fry for a few seconds, then add all the other ingredients except the cornstarch mixture. Bring to a boil, stir the cornstarch mixture and slowly add it to the wok. Reduce the heat and simmer until the Sauce thickens. Return the spareribs to the wok, stir to coat well with the Sauce. Remove from the heat, transfer to a serving plate and serve hot with plain rice.

Many people like to add canned pineapple chunks to this dish and you can use the juice from the pineapple in place of the 4 tablespoons of chicken stock or water in the Sauce.

Serves 4
Preparation time: 20 mins + marinating time
Cooking time: 20 mins

Star Anise Beef with Ginger

Beef is one of the most popular items on northern Chinese menus. Stewing is a favorite method to prepare beef. This recipe is especially tasty and easy to prepare and may be cooked well in advance and then reheated.

$1^1/_2$ lbs (700 g) beef sir-loin, brisket or shank
$8^1/_2$ cups (2 liters) water
3 star anise pods
2–3 tablespoons sugar
$^3/_4$ cup (190 ml) soy sauce
$^3/_4$ cup (190 ml) rice wine or sherry
3 tablespoons oil
4 green onions (scallions), cut into short lengths
6 slices ginger, smashed with the back of a knife
$1^1/_2$ teaspoons cornstarch dissolved in 3 tablespoons water

Serves 4–6
Preparation time: **15 mins**
Cooking time: **2 hours**

1 Cut the beef into cubes. Bring the water to a boil in a large pot, blanch the beef cubes for 2 minutes. Remove the beef and set aside to drain in a colander. Reserve the cooking water.

2 Skim away all the fat and foam from the water in which the beef was blanched. Add the star anise, sugar, soy sauce and rice wine or sherry, and return to a boil. Lower the heat and let the stock simmer.

3 Heat the oil in a wok until smoking, add the beef cubes, green onion and ginger. Stir-fry for 3 minutes. Transfer the contents to the simmering stock, cover with a lid, reduce to low heat and simmer for 2 hours or until the beef is very tender and the stock is reduced.

4 Add the cornstarch mixture to the pot, stir and simmer for another 2 minutes until the sauce thickens. Transfer the beef and the sauce to a large bowl and serve.

You may also prepare this dish with lamb loin or shanks. Chopped fresh coriander leaves (cilantro) may be added as a garnish. For a more pungent flavor, add one whole red finger-length chili, cut in half lengthwise, to the stew pot.

Mongolian Lamb with Garlic

Lamb is a major ingredient on northern Chinese menus, reflecting culinary influence from the steppes of Mongolia. Lamb warms the body, making it a popular choice in cold northern climates. Northern Chinese chefs always marinate the lamb first and cook it with plenty of garlic.

1 lb (500 g) boneless lamb loin, sliced across the grain into fine slivers
4 tablespoons oil
10 cloves garlic, finely sliced
3 green onions (scallions), cut into short sections
1 tablespoon soy sauce
1 tablespoon rice wine
2 teaspoons sesame oil
1/2 teaspoon salt
1/2 cup (25 g) chopped fresh coriander leaves (cilantro), to garnish

Marinade
1/2 teaspoon salt
1 1/2 teaspoons ground Sichuan pepper or black pepper
2 tablespoons soy sauce
2 teaspoons rice wine
1 teaspoon sesame oil
1 teaspoon sugar
1 teaspoon cornstarch

1 Place the lamb with all the Marinade ingredients in a bowl and mix well. Set aside to marinate for 20–30 minutes.
2 Heat the oil in a wok until smoking hot. Add the sliced garlic and marinated lamb. Stir-fry quickly for about 2 minutes or until the lamb changes color. Add the rest of the ingredients and stir-fry for 1 more minute. Transfer to a platter, garnish with the chopped coriander leaves and serve immediately.

Serves 2–3
Preparation time: 5 mins + 30 mins marinating time
Cooking time: 10 mins

Singapore Chili Crab

2 fresh crabs (about 2$^1/_2$ lbs/1.25 kg total)
2 tablespoons oil
6 small shallots, diced
6–8 cloves garlic, minced
3 tablespoons minced ginger
1 red finger-length chili, deseeded and sliced
3 cups (750 ml) Chinese Chicken Stock (page 8) or canned chicken stock
4 tablespoons black bean paste
4 tablespoons bottled sweet chili sauce
$^1/_2$ cup (125 ml) bottled tomato ketchup
1 tablespoon sugar
2 tablespoons rice wine
2 teaspoons salt
1 teaspoon pepper
2 tablespoons cornstarch mixed with 3 tablespoons water
2 eggs, lightly beaten
2 sprigs coriander leaves (cilantro), to garnish
2 green onions (scallions), to garnish
1 loaf of French bread

Chili Ginger Sauce
5–6 red finger-length chilies, deseeded
6 cloves garlic, peeled
4 slices fresh ginger
2 teaspoons sugar
$^1/_2$ teaspoon salt
1 teaspoon rice vinegar
1 tablespoon water

1 If the crabs are still alive, put them in the freezer for 15–20 minutes to immobilize them. Halve them lengthwise with a heavy cleaver, then remove the back and spongy grey matter. Pull the claws free and smash them in several places with a mallet. Cut each half of the body into 2–3 pieces, keeping the legs attached.

2 To make the Chili Ginger Sauce, blend all the ingredients in a mortar or blender. Set aside.

3 Heat the oil in a wok over medium heat and stir-fry the shallots, garlic, ginger and chili until fragrant, about 3 minutes. Add the Chili Ginger Sauce, Chinese Chicken Stock, black bean paste, chili sauce, tomato sauce, sugar, rice wine, salt and pepper, and bring to a boil. Then reduce the heat and simmer, for 2 minutes. Add the crabs and simmer uncovered, tossing several times until cooked, about 10 minutes.

4 Add the cornstarch mixture and stir the sauce until it thickens. Add the eggs and stir gently until they set, then transfer everything to a large serving dish. Garnish with fresh coriander leaves and green onions, and serve with slices of French bread on the side.

Serves 4–6
Preparation time: 1 hour
Cooking time: 20 mins

Flash-fried Garlic Shrimp

The shrimp in this dish are fried with the shells and heads left on—a traditional Chinese cooking method which not only preserves the natural flavor of the shrimp, but also locks in the juices. The blend of flavors here is a typically northern Chinese combination, with the accent on garlic.

4 tablespoons oil
20 large fresh shrimp (about 1²/₃ lbs/750 g total), shells and heads intact
6 cloves garlic, smashed with the flat side of a cleaver
3 slices fresh ginger, smashed
2 green onions (scallions), cut into lengths
1 tablespoon rice wine
1 teaspoon salt
1 teaspoon ground black pepper
2 tablespoons water

1 Heat the oil in a wok until smoking hot, add the shrimp and stir-fry for 3 minutes until they change color. Remove them from the wok, reserving the oil. Set the shrimp aside on a plate.
2 Fry the garlic, ginger and green onions in the reserved oil for 2–3 minutes to release the flavor and aroma into the oil, then remove and discard them.
3 Return the shrimp to the wok. Add the rest of the ingredients and stir-fry until most of the water has evaporated, about 2–3 minutes. Transfer to a serving platter and serve immediately.

Chopped fresh coriander leaves (cilantro) may be used as a garnish. For a more aromatic pungent flavor, ground Sichuan peppercorns may be used instead of the black pepper.

Serves 4–6
Preparation time: 20 mins
Cooking time: 10 mins

Shrimp with Sweet Chili Sauce

Shrimp are popular throughout the world, but no one cooks them better than the Chinese. In this Sichuan version, they are first marinated in ginger and rice wine, then cooked very quickly with garlic, green onions and a sweet chili sauce. For best results, use fresh shrimp, although frozen shrimp may also be used in a pinch.

1 1/2 lbs (700 g) large fresh shrimp, peeled and deveined
2 tablespoons oil
4 cloves garlic, chopped
4 green onions (scallions), cut into lengths

Marinade
2 tablespoons rice wine
1 teaspoon sesame oil
1 tablespoon minced ginger
1/2 teaspoon sugar

Sauce
2 tablespoons bottled sweet chili sauce
1 teaspoon bottled tomato ketchup
1/2 teaspoon sugar
1 teaspoon salt
1 teaspoon sesame oil
2 teaspoons cornstarch mixed with 1/2 cup (125 ml) water

1 Place the shrimp in a bowl. Add the Marinade ingredients and mix well with a spoon or using your fingers. Set aside to marinate for 15–20 minutes.
2 Combine the Sauce ingredients in a bowl and set aside.
3 Heat the oil in a wok until hot. Add the garlic and the marinated shrimp and stir-fry swiftly until the shrimp turn pink and the flesh becomes firm, about 1–2 minutes. Add the Sauce and stir-fry for a further 1 minute until it begins to thicken.
4 Add the green onions and cook for 30 seconds more, then transfer to a platter and serve immediately.

You may lessen the heat of the chili by using just 1 tablespoon of chili sauce. As with most Sichuan seafood dishes, chopped fresh coriander leaves (cilantro) makes an excellent garnish. You may also use this recipe to prepare fresh or frozen scallops or fish fillets cut into bite-sized chunks.

Serves 4
Preparation time: 30 mins + marinating time
Cooking time: 5 mins

Shrimp or Lobster with Snow Peas

This quick and easy stir-fry can also be made with fresh lobster meat for a wonderful indulgence.

1 1/2 lbs (700 g) large fresh shrimp, peeled and deveined or 8 oz (250 g) fresh lobster meat
2 tablespoons oil
1 cup (80 g) snow peas, trimmed
1/4 teaspoon salt
Pinch of sugar
4 cloves garlic, minced
1/2 tablespoon grated ginger
1/2 tablespoon soy sauce
1 tablespoon rice wine or sherry
1 tablespoon chicken stock or water
1/2 tablespoon chili bean paste
2 tablespoons bottled tomato ketchup

Marinade
1 teaspoon cornstarch, blended with 1/4 cup (60 ml) water
1 egg white
1/2 teaspoon sugar
1/4 teaspoon salt

1 Combine the shrimp or lobster meat with the Marinade ingredients in a mixing bowl. Massage the shrimp or lobster gently, to mix well. Set aside to marinate for 10–15 minutes.

2 Heat 1 tablespoon of oil in a wok until very hot, then add the snow peas, salt and a pinch of sugar. Stir-fry for 1 minute, then remove the snow peas and set aside.

3 Heat the remaining oil in a wok until very hot, then stir-fry the marinated shrimp or lobster meat for 1 minute. Add the garlic and ginger, stirring to mix thoroughly. Add the soy sauce, rice wine, chicken stock, chili bean paste and tomato ketchup. Continue to stir-fry until the shrimp or lobster meat is cooked. Remove from the heat and serve hot.

Serves 4
Preparation time: 15 mins + marinating time
Cooking time: 10 mins

Crystal Shrimp with Asparagus

1 lb (500 g) fresh shrimp, peeled and deveined
1 teaspoon baking soda
4 teaspoons cornstarch
$^1/_2$ teaspoon salt
1 teaspoon sugar
1 egg white, whisked
2 tablespoons oil
1 teaspoon chopped ginger
$^1/_2$ lb (250 g) fresh young asparagus, trimmed and sliced

Sauce
$^1/_2$ cup (125 ml) chicken stock or water
1 tablespoon rice wine
1 tablespoon oyster sauce
1 teaspoon cornstarch

1 Place the peeled shrimp in a bowl and sprinkle with the baking soda and cornstarch. Massage by hand for 2 minutes to coat well. Sprinkle the salt and sugar over the shrimp, then stir in the egg white. Mix well and set aside to marinate for 5 minutes. Drain and set aside

2 Combine the Sauce ingredients in a bowl. Set aside.

3 Heat the oil in a wok. Add the ginger and stir-fry for 10 seconds. Add the asparagus and stir-fry for 1 minute. Add the shrimp and stir-fry over high heat until just cooked, 2–3 minutes.

4 Stir the Sauce mixture then add it to the wok. Lower the heat slightly and stir until the Sauce thickens and clears, about 30 seconds. Remove from the heat and serve immediately.

Serves 4
Preparation time: 15 mins
Cooking time: 5 mins

Clams Baked with Rice Wine

The clams used in this recipe are the larger variety, 1–1¹/₂ in (3–4 cm) in diameter, not the smaller ones used in soups and stir-fries. The clams must be absolutely fresh when purchased and should be cooked on the same day.

2 lbs (1 kg) fresh clams in the shell
2 tablespoons rice wine
2 tablespoons salt
¹/₂ cup (20 g) chopped fresh basil leaves
¹/₂ cup (30 g) chopped iceberg lettuce

Serves 2–4
Preparation time: 5 mins + 30 mins soaking
Cooking time: 12 mins

1 Preheat the oven to 400°F (200°C).
2 Scrub and clean the clams well. Soak in lightly salted water for 30 minutes to remove any sand trapped within the clams. Rinse in a couple of changes of water and drain.
3 Arrange the clams on a baking dish and brush the shells with some wine, then sprinkle them with the salt, making sure that the salt sticks to the shells.
4 Bake the clams in the oven for 10–12 minutes, until the shells have all opened. Remove from the oven.
5 Mix the chopped basil and lettuce on a serving platter, then arrange the baked clams on top. Serve immediately.

Sweet and Sour Sliced Fish

Oil, for deep-frying
1¼ lbs (600 g) white
 fish fillets, cut into thick
 slices
1 teaspoon salt
¼ teaspoon pepper
1 egg, lightly beaten
½ cup (80 g) plain flour
Fresh coriander leaves
 (cilantro) and lettuce
 leaves, to garnish

Sweet and Sour Sauce
1–2 red finger-length
 chilies, deseeded
4 cloves garlic
4 slices fresh ginger
2 tablespoons oil
2 fresh tomatoes, diced
½ cup (125 ml) water
2 tablespoons bottled
 tomato ketchup
2 tablespoons rice vine-
 gar or lemon juice
2 tablespoons soy sauce
1 tablespoon sugar
1 teaspoon salt
1 tablespoon cornstarch
1 tablespoon water

1 To prepare the Sweet and Sour Sauce, process the chilies, garlic and ginger to a smooth paste in a mortar or blender adding a little oil if necessary to keep the mixture turning. Heat the oil in a saucepan and add the chili mixture. Stir-fry over low-medium heat until fragrant, about 4 minutes.
2 Add the diced tomatoes and cook, stirring frequently, until they are reduced to a pulp, 5-6 minutes. Add the water, tomato ketchup, vinegar or lemon juice, soy sauce, sugar and salt. Bring to a boil, stirring, and simmer for 2 minutes.
3 Combine the cornstarch and water in a small bowl, then add to the Sauce and cook, stirring, until the Sauce thickens, about 30 seconds. Keep the Sauce warm over very low heat while the cooking the fish.
4 Heat the oil for deep-drying in a wok. Pat the fish fillets dry with paper towels then sprinkle them on both sides with the salt and pepper. Dip the fish fillets, one at a time, into the beaten egg and then dredge in the flour, making sure the fillets are completely covered. Shake to remove any excess flour, then gently drop the fish fillets into the hot oil and deep-fry until cooked through and golden brown, 3–4 minutes. Remove and place on a serving dish and pour the Sweet and Sour Sauce over the fish just before serving. Serve on a bed of lettuce leaves and garnish with fresh coriander leaves.

Serves 4
Preparation time: **20 mins**
Cooking time: **25 mins**

Pan-fried Fish Steaks

3 fish steaks, total about 14 oz (400 g), cleaned and patted dry with paper towels
3 tablespoons oil
2 slices fresh ginger, cut into thin matchsticks
2 green onions (scallions), cut into short lengths
2 cloves garlic, sliced
1 tablespoon rice wine
3/4 cup (200 ml) fish stock or water
1 teaspoon dark soy sauce
1 tablespoon sugar
1 tablespoon rice vinegar
1 teaspoon sesame oil
1 red finger-length chili, deseeded and sliced
1 sprig fresh coriander leaves (cilantro), to garnish

Marinade
1 teaspoon five spice powder
1 tablespoon ginger juice (page 32)
2 tablespoons soy sauce
1 tablespoon sugar
1/4 teaspoon pepper

1 Combine the Marinade ingredients in a bowl and stir well until the sugar completely dissolves. Place the fish steaks in the Marinade and set aside to marinate for 30 minutes, turning the fish every 10 minutes. Drain; reserving the Marinade for the gravy.

2 Heat 2 tablespoons of the oil in a wok or skillet. Very carefully slide in the fish and fry until golden brown on both sides. Transfer to a serving dish.

3 Clean the pan, add the remaining 1 tablespoon of oil, and stir-fry the ginger, green onions and garlic until aromatic.

4 Sizzle in the wine, then add the reserved fish marinade and stock or water. Bring to a boil and stir in the dark soy sauce and sugar. Return the fish to the pan and simmer over low heat in the sauce for 5–6 minutes.

5 When the sauce is nearly dry, sprinkle in the vinegar and sesame oil. Mix well, remove from the heat and transfer to a serving dish. Garnish with sliced chilies and fresh coriander leaves and serve hot.

Serves 2
Preparation time: 40 mins
Cooking time: 20 mins

Fish Steamed with Wine and Soy

1 whole pomfret or other white fish, cleaned or 1$^1/_2$ lbs (700 g) fresh fish fillets
$^1/_2$ teaspoon salt
$^1/_2$ teaspoon sugar
1 tablespoon soy sauce
2 teaspoons rice wine
1$^1/_2$ in (4 cm) fresh ginger, peeled and sliced into slivers
2 dried black Chinese mushrooms, soaked in warm water for 20 minutes, tough stems discarded and caps thinly sliced
2 green onions (scallions), cut into short lengths
2 teaspoons oil
1 teaspoon sesame oil
2 bottled sour plums (*sin mui*) or $^1/_3$ cup (50 g) thinly-sliced salted pickled mustard cabbage (*kiam chye*)
Pinch of pepper
Fresh coriander leaves (cilantro), to garnish

1 Make diagonal slits on both sides of the fish. Place the fish on a plate and rub the salt and sugar on both sides. Drizzle the soy sauce and rice wine over the fish and set aside to marinate for 15 minutes.
2 Scatter half the ginger, mushrooms and green onions on a heatproof dish, then place the fish with the marinade over it. Scatter the remaining ginger, mushrooms and green onions over the fish and drizzle the oil and sesame oil on top. Place the sour plums or salted pickled cabbage on the fish and put the plate on a steaming rack inside a wok or steamer, half-filled with boiling water.
3 Cover and steam the fish over high heat until cooked, about 10–15 minutes depending on the size and thickness of the fish. Add more boiling water as needed. The flesh should be white to the bone when fully cooked. Season with pepper and garnish with fresh coriander leaves. Serve hot.

Serves 4
Preparation time: 10 mins + marinating time
Cooking time: 15–25 mins

Garlic Eggplant

2–3 long Asian eggplants
Oil, for deep-frying
2 cloves garlic, minced
1 teaspoon sesame oil

Sauce
1 tablespoon soy sauce
2 green onions (scallions),
   cut into lengths
1 teaspoon salt
2 slices fresh ginger,
   minced
2 tablespoons cornstarch
   dissolved in 2 table-
   spoons water
6 tablespoons water

1 Peel and halve the eggplants lengthwise then slice them into bite-sized pieces.

2 Heat the oil in a wok over high heat. Add the eggplant slices and deep-fry them until the eggplant turns brown. Remove and drain on paper towels. Pour out the oil, reserving about 2 tablespoons of oil in the wok.

3 Combine all the Sauce ingredients in a bowl, stirring to mix well. Set aside.

4 Heat the reserved oil in the wok over high heat. Add the garlic and fry until fragrant. Return the eggplant slices to the wok. Slowly stir in the Sauce. Bring the Sauce to a boil and simmer, stirring, until the Sauce thickens. Drizzle the sesame oil into the pan, remove from the heat and serve immediately.

Serves 4–6
Preparation time: **10 mins**
Cooking time: **10 mins**

Poached Bok Choy with Oyster Sauce

1 lb (500 g) *bok choy*, cut
in half lengthwise
8 cloves garlic, finely
chopped and fried in a
little oil till golden brown
2 tablespoons soy sauce
1 tablespoon oyster sauce
1 teaspoon sugar
1 teaspoon sesame oil

Serves 4–6
Preparation time: 20 mins
Cooking time: 20 mins

1 Poach the *bok choy* in a pot of boiling water for 2–3 minutes. Remove and set aside to drain in a colander.
2 Mix the rest of the ingredients in a small bowl to make a sauce. Arrange the vegetables on a serving dish. Drizzle the sauce over and serve immediately.

Fresh oysters make a delicious addition to this dish. Place 10–15 freshly shucked oysters with 1 teaspoon salt in a bowl. Toss to mix and drain well in a colander. Place the drained oysters with 1 tablespoon cornstarch in a bowl and toss to mix evenly. Poach the oysters in boiling water until the cornstarch coating becomes translucent and shiny, about 2–3 minutes. Arrange the vegetables in a fan shape, with the leaves toward the center. Place the oysters on top of the vegetables before drizzling the sauce over them.

Tofu with Pork and Black Bean Sauce

2 cakes tofu (about 10 oz/300 g each)

$^{1}/_{4}$ cup (60 ml) oil

1 tablespoon dried shrimp, soaked in warm water, drained and chopped in a blender

2 tablespoons black bean sauce (see note)

2 green onions (scallions), chopped

3 slices fresh ginger

2 cloves garlic, chopped

$^{1}/_{2}$ cup (100 g) ground pork

5 tablespoons soy sauce

2 tablespoons rice wine

$^{1}/_{2}$ cup (125 ml) chicken stock

1 tablespoon cornstarch dissolved in 1 tablespoon of water

2 tablespoons chopped fresh coriander leaves (cilantro), to garnish

Sichuan Pepper Oil

2 tablespoons Sichuan peppercorns

8 tablespoons oil

Serves 4–6
Preparation time: **10 mins**
Cooking time: **20 mins**

1 Make the Sichuan Pepper Oil by heating a skillet over medium heat. Reduce the heat to low and add the Sichuan peppercorns. Dry-roast the peppercorns, shaking the pan occasionally, until they are aromatic. Set aside to cool. Crush the peppercorns with a mortar or coarsely blend them in a food processor. Heat the oil in a separate pan over high heat. Turn off the heat and add the crushed peppercorns to the oil. Set aside to cool. Strain the flavored oil and store in a sealed jar at room temperature.

2 Place the tofu in a heat-proof bowl and steam for 10 minutes. Remove, drain and cut into small cubes. Place them on a serving platter and set aside.

3 Heat the oil in a wok over high heat. Add the chopped dried shrimp, black bean sauce, green onion, ginger, garlic and ground pork. Stir-fry for 2 minutes. Add the soy sauce, rice wine and chicken stock. Stir in the cornstarch mixture and cook, stirring, until the sauce thickens.

4 Remove from the heat and pour the mixture over the tofu cubes. Garnish with chopped fresh coriander leaves and drizzle a bit of the Sichuan Pepper Oil over the dish before serving.

Black bean sauce is a richly-flavored seasoning made from fermented black beans (also called salted black beans). It is sold in jars and can be found in the international section of most supermarkets.

Stir-fried Chinese Greens

1 lb (500 g) Chinese greens, such as *bok choy* or *kailan* or flowering cabbage (*choy sum*), washed and sliced
2 tablespoons minced garlic
1 teaspoon minced ginger
1 tablespoon oil
$1/2$ teaspoon salt
1 teaspoon sesame oil

1 Soak and rinse the vegetables, trimming away any bruised or hard bits. If the leaves are too large, cut them into smaller pieces.
2 Heat the oil in a wok or skillet and stir-fry the minced garlic and ginger with the salt until fragrant. Add the vegetables, cover with the lid and cook for $1/2$–1 minute.
3 Remove the lid and toss to mix evenly until thoroughly cooked, about 2 minutes. Drizzle in the sesame oil and serve hot.

Serves 2
Preparation time: **20 mins**
Cooking time: **8 mins**

Blanched Chinese Greens with Chili and Garlic

1 teaspoon salt
1 teaspoon oil
1 lb (500 g) Chinese
greens, such as *bok
choy* or *kailan* or flowering cabbage (*choy sum*),
washed and drained
(see note)

Sauce
2 tablespoons soy sauce
1 teaspoon sugar
1 teaspoon dark soy sauce
1 tablespoon sesame oil
$1/_2$ teaspoon ground
Sichuan pepper
2 red finger-length chilies,
deseeded and chopped
2 cloves garlic, minced

1 Combine the Sauce ingredients in a bowl and set aside.
2 Bring a pot of water to a rolling boil, add the salt
and oil to the water, then add the vegetables. When
the water has returned to a boil, remove the vegetables, rinse in cold running water to set the color, then
drain well.
3 Arrange the cooked vegetables on a serving platter,
then pour the mixed Sauce evenly on top and serve.

Choy sum or **chye sim**, also known as Chinese greens
or Chinese flowering cabbage, is a leafy green
vegetable with crisp crunchy stems. Available in supermarkets in Asia, it is now increasingly available in
Western countries too.

Serves 4
Preparation time: **10 mins**
Cooking time: **2 mins**

Stir-fried Mixed Chinese Vegetables

8 dried black Chinese mushrooms

$^3/_4$ cup (60 g) canned or fresh baby corns

1 cup (100 g) whole button mushrooms

1 tablespoon oil

$^1/_4$ teaspoon salt

1 cup (100 g) cauliflower florets

$^1/_2$ cup (50 g) sliced carrot

1 cup (100 g) broccoli florets

$^1/_3$ cup (80 ml) chicken stock

1 teaspoon soy sauce

2 tablespoons oyster sauce

$^1/_2$ teaspoon sugar

1 teaspoon sesame oil

1 Soak the dried mushrooms in warm water for 15 minutes to soften, then drain and discard the tough stems. Slice the caps.

2 Bring a small pan of water to a boil and blanch the baby corn and the button mushrooms, then rinse.

3 Heat the oil in a wok. Add the salt, cauliflower and carrot and stir-fry for 2 minutes. Add the baby corn, broccoli and mushrooms. Stir to combine.

4 Pour in the stock and continue cooking for 1 minute. Season with soy sauce, oyster sauce, sugar and sesame oil, and adjust the flavor to taste. Serve hot.

Serves 2–4
Preparation time: **20 mins**
Cooking time: **20 mins**

Chinese Broccoli with Salted Fish and Ginger

14 oz (400 g) baby *kailan*, halved or 1 lb (500 g) broccoli, cut into florets
3 tablespoons oil
3 tablespoons salted fish, chopped, soaked in hot water and drained
1 in (2.5 cm) fresh ginger, thinly sliced into slivers
$1/_2$ teaspoon salt
1 teaspoon soy sauce
1 tablespoon rice wine
3 tablespoons chicken stock or 1 tablespoon oyster sauce

1 Wash and rinse the baby *kailan*, discarding the outer leaves if they are hard. Trim off the bottom $1/_4$ in (6 mm) of the stalks. If using broccoli, wash and slice, discarding the tough stems.

2 Heat the oil in a skillet over high heat. Reduce the heat to medium, stir-fry the salted fish until crisp, about 6–10 minutes, then remove from the pan and set aside.

3 Stir-fry the ginger for about one minute, then add the *kailan* or broccoli, salt, soy sauce, rice wine and chicken stock or oyster sauce. Stir-fry for 5–7 minutes over high heat.

4 Add the reserved salted fish, stir quickly, then transfer to a serving plate and serve hot with rice.

Serves 4
Preparation time: 20 mins
Cooking time: 30 mins

Complete Recipe Listing